MW01515346

WRITING WORKBOOK for kids with Dyslexia

100 activities to improve writing and reading skills of dyslexic children

Volume 3

BrainChild

Table of Contents

Copyright 2020 - All Rights Reserved

Contents of this book may not be reproduced, duplicated or transmitted without direct written permission from the author. Under no circumstances will any legal responsibility or blame be held against the publisher for any reparation, damages or monetary loss due to information herein, either directly or indirectly.

Legal Notice

You cannot amend, distribute, sell, use, quote or paraphrase any part of the contents within this book without the consent of the author.

Disclaimer Notice

Please note that information contained within this document serves only for educational and entertainment purposes only. No warranties of any kind are expressed or implied. Readers acknowledge that the author is not engaging in the rendering of legal, financial, medical or professional advice.

INTRODUCTION

Dyslexia is a learning disorder. It can be said that a person is dyslexic when they have difficulties reading and understanding what is written. When a child has dyslexia, it is much more difficult to decode the letters and read fluently that is why these children often lose the thread of the class. Dyslexia can be worked to improve the child's reading, writing, and comprehension.

The best way to work on these exercises with your child is to create a routine and work on one or two exercises each day. In this volume, we cover exercises to practice writing with a complementary activity to also practice with the letters learned. Never put excessive pressure on the child. Patience should be our word mantra. Keep in mind that for the child an exercise that you consider easy is very hard for them.

Focus on the child's small advances. Power your effort and less your results. Do everything you can so that they don't feel bad. Keep in mind that the child is making a great effort. When we suspect that our child may be dyslexic, we can do a series of activities that will improve his literacy level. Whether in the end, the diagnosis is confirmed or discarded, it will still be very beneficial to facilitate their learning experience.

INTRODUCTION

The important thing is to carry out this type of training before the age of 8 or 9, preferably during the last year of preschool and the first year of Primary School, without taking into account that from school there is still no warning. In any case, we cannot wait for the diagnosis to be confirmed because we will have missed the best time to intervene and prepare the child to learn to read, and we will have a serious problem if they start 3rd grade and we have not yet intervened the dyslexia, since the increase in school demands will make the problem visible.

In this book and the other volumes of BrainChild, you will find a multitude of resources to work with dyslexia both at school and at home. The exercises have been carried out under the supervision of psychologists and educators.

Press the dot and say the sound of each letter

Press the dot and say the sound of each letter, then move your fingers across the arrow and blend the sound to read the word

ant art axe ask act

Trace the letter A and continue writing on the second line

Finger trace the letter

Color the objects that begin with the letter B

Press the dot and say the sound of each letter

a e x b o w d t

Press the dot and say the sound of each letter, then move your fingers across the arrow and blend the sound to read the word

bat box bow bed bad

Trace the letter B and continue writing on the second line

Finger trace the letter

Press the dot and say the sound of each letter

 t o r c u n p w

Press the dot and say the sound of each letter, then move your fingers across the arrow and blend the sound to read the word

cat car cup can cow

Trace the letter C and continue writing on the second line

Finger trace the letter

Color the objects that begin with the letter D

Press the dot and say the sound of each letter

d o u a p t g i

Press the dot and say the sound of each letter, then move your fingers across the arrow and blend the sound to read the word

dot dad dug dip dog

Trace the letter D and continue writing on the second line

Press the dot and say the sound of each letter

l f n e d k g t

Press the dot and say the sound of each letter, then move your fingers across the arrow and blend the sound to read the word

elf egg end elk eat

Trace the letter E and continue writing on the second line

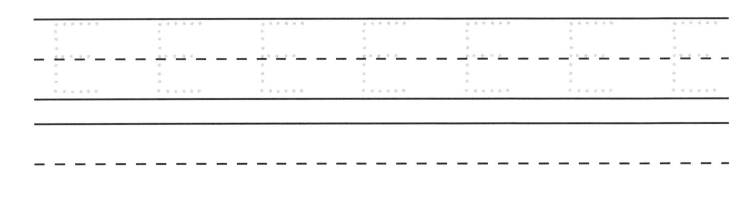

Finger trace the letter

Color the objects that begin with the letter F

Press the dot and say the sound of each letter

 f

i f o a e d x n

Press the dot and say the sound of each letter, then move your fingers across the arrow and blend the sound to read the word

fit fat fox fed fun

Trace the letter F and continue writing on the second line

Finger trace the letter

Press the dot and say the sound of each letter

     g i

Press the dot and say the sound of each letter, then move your fingers across the arrow and blend the sound to read the word

gun gut gap gig gum

Trace the letter G and continue writing on the second line

Hh

Press the dot and say the sound of each letter

Press the dot and say the sound of each letter, then move your fingers across the arrow and blend the sound to read the word

hot hat hen ham hid

Trace the letter H and continue writing on the second line

Finger trace the letter

Color the objects that begin with the letter I

Press the dot and say the sound of each letter

i k n v y t l c

Press the dot and say the sound of each letter, then move your fingers across the arrow and blend the sound to read the word

ink ice ivy ill it

Trace the letter I and continue writing on the second line

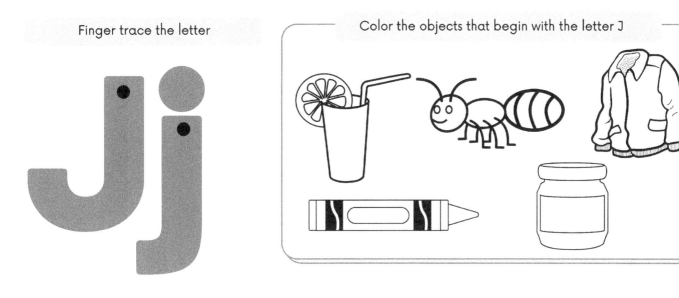

Press the dot and say the sound of each letter

i k n v y t l c

Press the dot and say the sound of each letter, then move your fingers across the arrow and blend the sound to read the word

jam jug jaw job jet

Trace the letter J and continue writing on the second line

_____

- -

_____

- -

_____

Kk

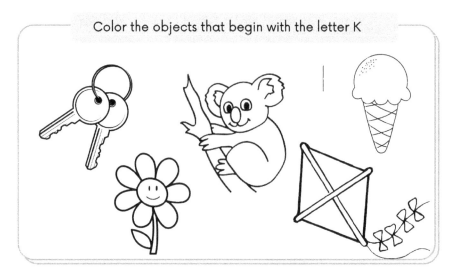

Press the dot and say the sound of each letter

i k t e s y

Press the dot and say the sound of each letter, then move your fingers across the arrow and blend the sound to read the word

key kit kiss kite

Trace the letter K and continue writing on the second line

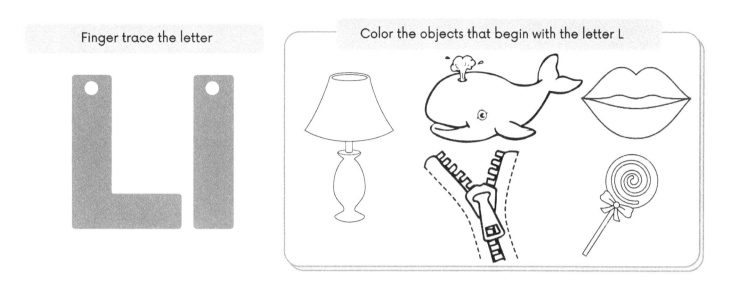

Press the dot and say the sound of each letter

Press the dot and say the sound of each letter, then move your fingers across the arrow and blend the sound to read the word

log leg lid lamp

Trace the letter L and continue writing on the second line

Press the dot and say the sound of each letter

Press the dot and say the sound of each letter, then move your fingers across the arrow and blend the sound to read the word

man mad mug mat mop

Trace the letter M and continue writing on the second line

Press the dot and say the sound of each letter

p a n e o w b t

Press the dot and say the sound of each letter, then move your fingers across the arrow and blend the sound to read the word

nap not net now nib

Trace the letter N and continue writing on the second line

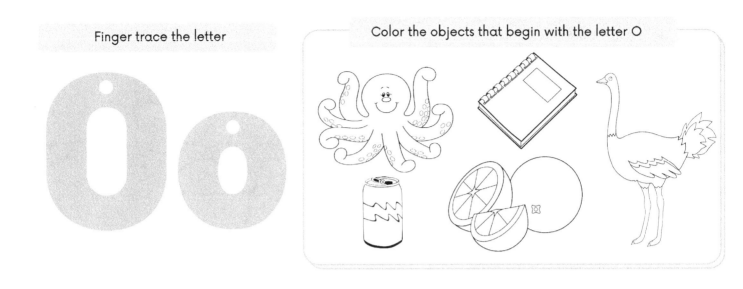

Press the dot and say the sound of each letter

o l e d w n w

Press the dot and say the sound of each letter, then move your fingers across the arrow and blend the sound to read the word

own owl old odd one

Trace the letter O and continue writing on the second line

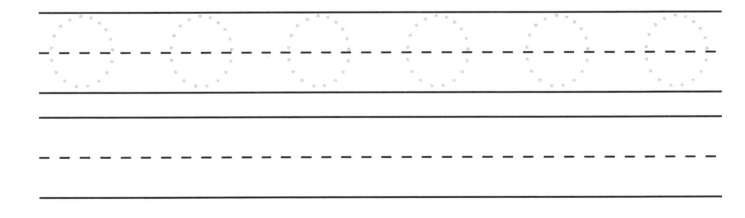

Press the dot and say the sound of each letter

p n o i g a e t

Press the dot and say the sound of each letter, then move your fingers across the arrow and blend the sound to read the word

pot pan pig pin pen

Trace the letter P and continue writing on the second line

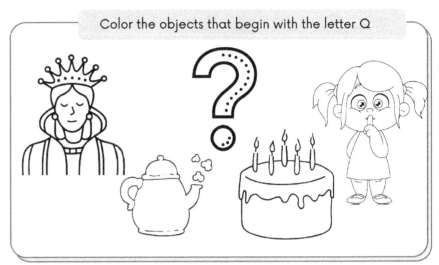

Press the dot and say the sound of each letter

q t u i a e l n

Press the dot and say the sound of each letter, then move your fingers across the arrow and blend the sound to read the word

queen quiet quail

Trace the letter Q and continue writing on the second line

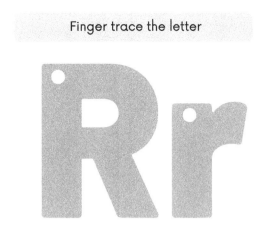

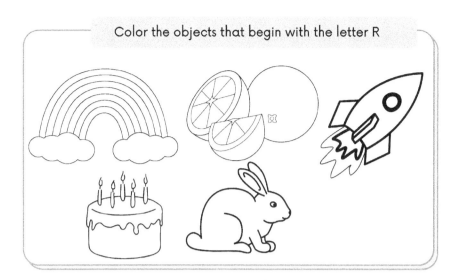

Press the dot and say the sound of each letter

d r a e u n o b

Press the dot and say the sound of each letter, then move your fingers across the arrow and blend the sound to read the word

red rod rat rub run

Trace the letter R and continue writing on the second line

S s

Press the dot and say the sound of each letter

a   s   w   e   u   x   n   t

Press the dot and say the sound of each letter, then move your fingers across the arrow and blend the sound to read the word

sat sun saw sew six

Trace the letter S and continue writing on the second line

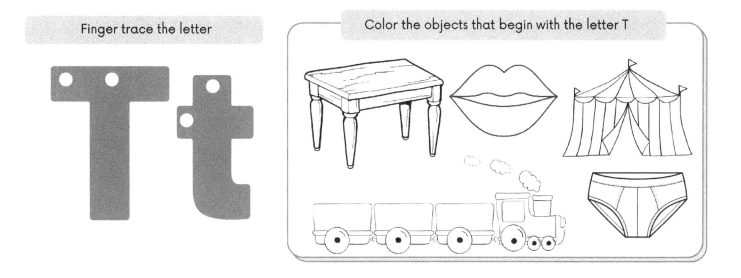

Press the dot and say the sound of each letter

i n w e o t a

Press the dot and say the sound of each letter, then move your fingers across the arrow and blend the sound to read the word

tin tan ten two tow

Trace the letter T and continue writing on the second line

Finger trace the letter

U u

Color the objects that begin with the letter U

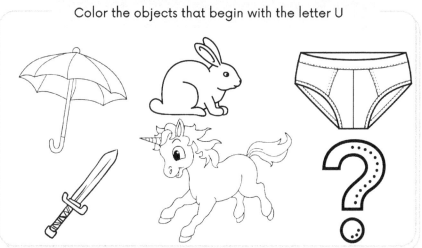

Press the dot and say the sound of each letter

u n e r c l y d

Press the dot and say the sound of each letter, then move your fingers across the arrow and blend the sound to read the word

ugly uncle under

Trace the letter U and continue writing on the second line

Vv

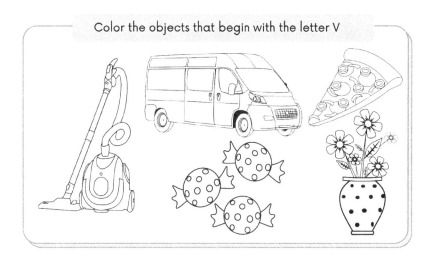

Press the dot and say the sound of each letter

v e w o n i a t

Press the dot and say the sound of each letter, then move your fingers across the arrow and blend the sound to read the word

van vet vow vat vine

Trace the letter V and continue writing on the second line

_____

- -

_____

_____

- -

_____

Finger trace the letter

Color the objects that begin with the letter W

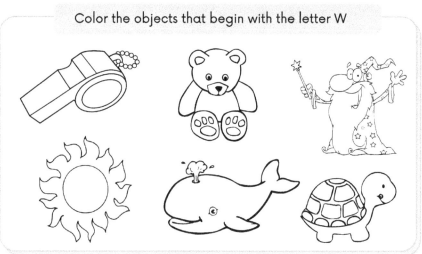

Press the dot and say the sound of each letter

Press the dot and say the sound of each letter, then move your fingers across the arrow and blend the sound to read the word

was wet won web win

Trace the letter W and continue writing on the second line

Finger trace the letter

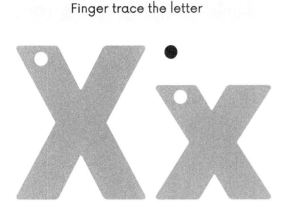

Color the objects that begin/ends with the letter X

Press the dot and say the sound of each letter

 f   x   s   i   a   o   b

Press the dot and say the sound of each letter, then move your fingers across the arrow and blend the sound to read the word

box fix ox six sax

Trace the letter X and continue writing on the second line

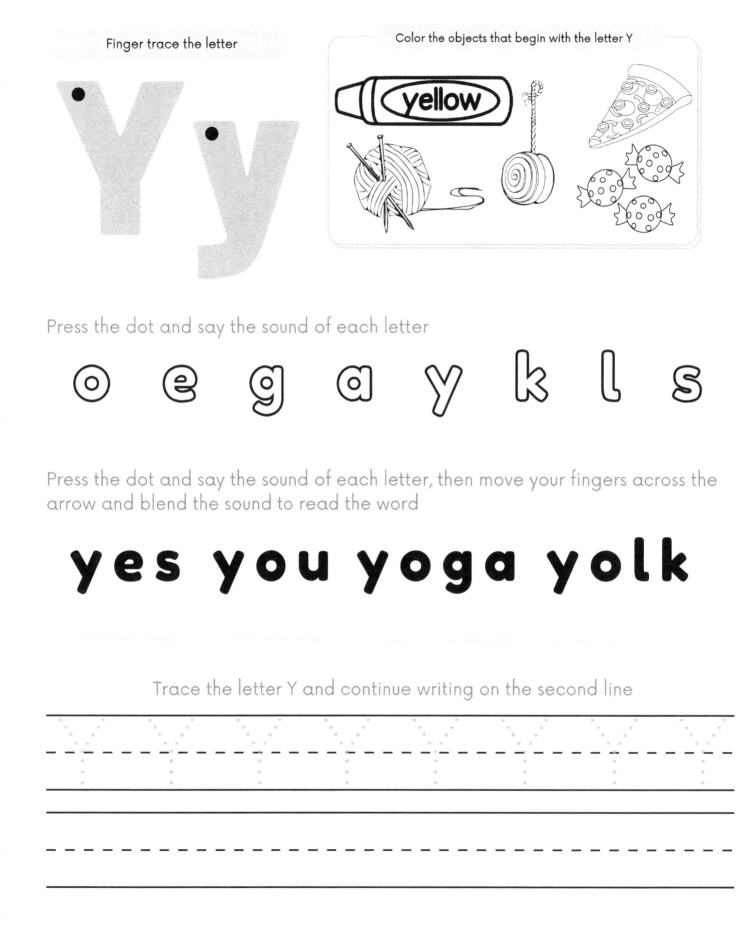

Y y

yellow

Press the dot and say the sound of each letter

o e g a y k l s

Press the dot and say the sound of each letter, then move your fingers across the arrow and blend the sound to read the word

yes you yoga yolk

Trace the letter Y and continue writing on the second line

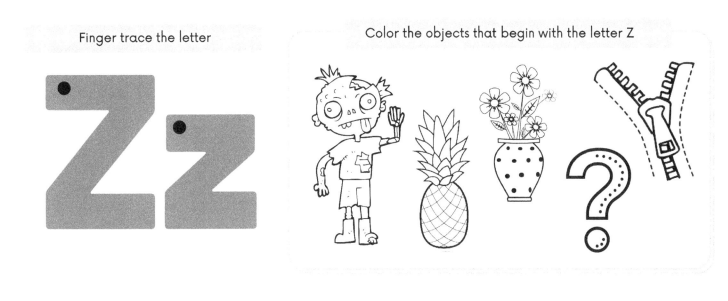

Press the dot and say the sound of each letter

p m o e z a r

Press the dot and say the sound of each letter, then move your fingers across the arrow and blend the sound to read the word

zoo zap zero zoom

Trace the letter Z and continue writing on the second line

SOUND IT OUT

Listen to each sound found in the following words.
Write each sounds on its given line.

example

BAG   _B_   _A_   _G_ | _BAG_ |

....

CAT   ___   ___   ___   _____

HAM   ___   ___   ___   _____

DOT   ___   ___   ___   _____

RUG   ___   ___   ___   _____

FIT   ___   ___   ___   _____

SUN   ___   ___   ___   _____

MAD   ___   ___   ___   _____

TAG   ___   ___   ___   _____

MUD

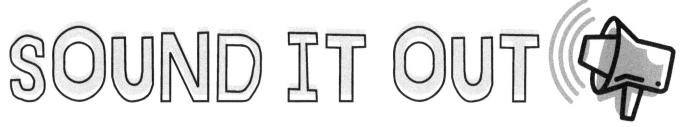

SOUND IT OUT

Listen to each sound found in the following words. Write each sounds on its given line. Digraphs make one sound so remember to keep those letters together on their sound line

example
PATH   P   A   TH   **PATH**

- -

CHIP ___ ___ ___   _____

FISH ___ ___ ___   _____

THAT ___ ___ ___   _____

SHED ___ ___ ___   _____

BATH ___ ___ ___   _____

QUIT ___ ___ ___   _____

WITH ___ ___ ___   _____

WHIP ___ ___ ___   _____

PUSH ___ ___ ___   _____

Using the U sound

Name a picture and choose one circle for each sound you hear

Color the circle that represents the U sound to match the picture below

A
short U
umbrella

B
long U
unicorn

C
long U
glue

Juice

(A) (B) (C)

Cube

(A) (B) (C)

Blue

(A) (B) (C)

Cut

(A) (B) (C)

Fruit

(A) (B) (C)

Cute

(A) (B) (C)

Magic E

Read each word → Change the word by adding E at the end. Now it follows the CVCe pattern and the first vowel is long. $\underline{e}$ → Draw a line to the picture that matches the new word

---

rob rob_

dim dim_

kit   kit_

tub tub_

man man_

Grandma's Groceries

1. Trace the letter while you say "/gr/ green grapes" three times.
2. Starting from the grandma. Name the picture next to her.
3. Color the box if the first sound of the word is /gr/. Make a path of colored squares until you reach the grocery store.

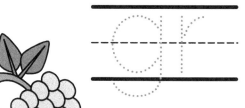

gr

/gr/
green
grapes

Begins with /bl/

1. Trace the letter while you say "/bl/ blocks" three times.
2. Name the picture in the first column.
3. Change the beginning sound of the picture in the first column to /bl/ and draw a line to the picture with the new word in the second column

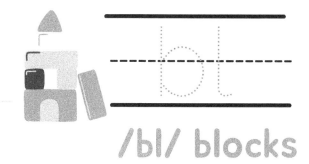

/bl/ blocks

broom

cast

chimp

hush

blush

bloom

blast

blimp

Splitting Sounds

1. Say the name of the object in each picture.

2. Split the word into its beginning sound and its ending sound. Touch the first box as you say the beginning sound, and the second box as you say the second sound

 _____ _____

_____ _____

_____ _____

_____ _____

_____ _____

_____ _____

_____ _____

Animals on the Go

1. Say the name of the animal
2. Draw a line to connect the animal to the picture that rhymes

Listen and Race

1. Listen to the sentences.
2. Repeat the sentences, and count the number of words
3. Color one box for each word that is said.
4. After all the sentences have been read and counted, the animal with the longest path is the winner of the race

Listen to the sentence.

Count the words.

Color the boxes.

The monkey ran fast.
The turtle tried his best.
The crab zoomed down the track.

The snail stopped.
The mouse got scared.

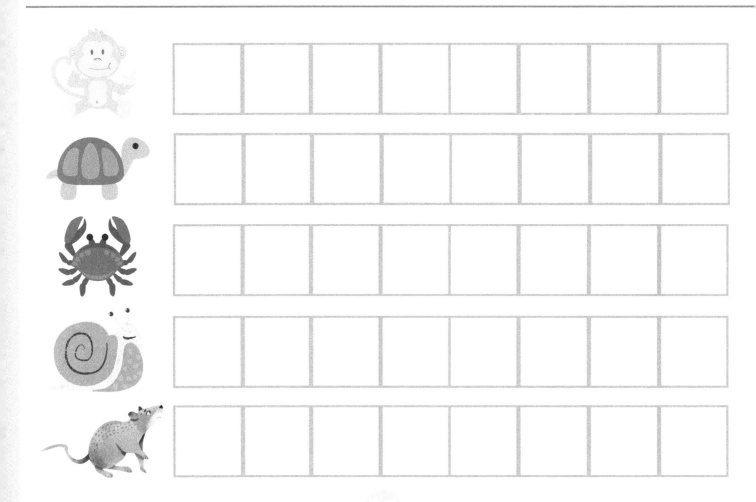

Slide Through the Circle

Blend the sounds together to make a word.
Circle the picture that matches the word.

cash

sheep

fish

shed

ship

-at Word Family

Color the circle that belongs to the -at family

−ap Word Family

Color the circle that belongs to the −ap family

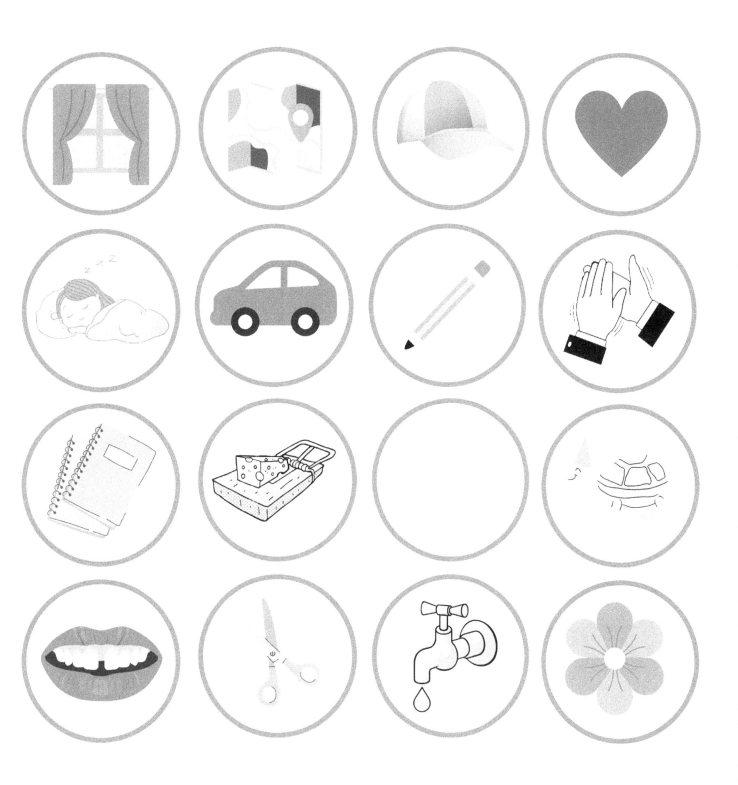

Rhyme Bubbles

Color the rhyming bubbles

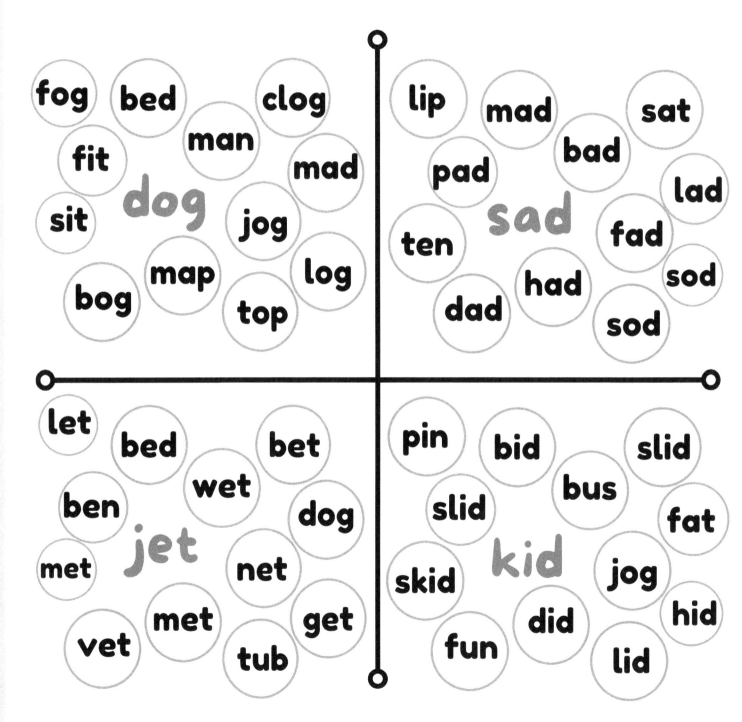

Beginning Digraphs

Look at the picture and say the word. Listen for the beginning digraph. Write the missing letters

eese

ark

ark

erry

air

orn

umb

ell

ale

Blends Matching

Draw a line from each picture to
the correct beginning blend

sh

sl

cr

sn

fr

bl

sp

br

cl

sw

Missing Sound

Write the missing beginning sound

	a	m

	u	n

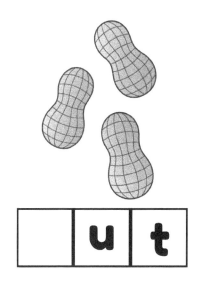

	u	t

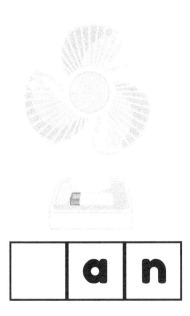

	a	n

	e	n

	u	s

Matching Words

Say the name of the picture. Read each word in the choices. Color the circle that matches the name of the picture

slide	sled	sly
pot	fat	pat
fat	pat	pot
fax	fox	tax
bat	but	bus

Find & Color
Rhyming Words

Circle the two pictures in each box that rhyme

Which word fits the picture? Color the box with the correct word

bik   bike

hive   hiv

rose   ros

cupe   cup

cake   cak

bede   bed

THROW A DIGRAPH

Look at each picture. Fill in the snowball with the correct digraph.

ma

○ elf

○ op

○ ick

tra

○ ess

slo

○ est

○ eck

○ ief

○ ark

ba

/SH/ DIGRAPHS

Highlight all the /sh/ words and write them next to their matching picture

shell	chap	bush	cash	such
shovel	sheep	sock	chair	brush
spin	sick	ship	shark	stick

Beginning Sounds

Say the name of each picture. Circle the letter of the beginning sound that you hear.

b d p   v g b   t s c   b e f

b h d   e k a   g c r   s b p

p t a   k c q   r d p   k c g

Beginning Blends

Say the name of each picture. Fill in the letters that make the beginning sound

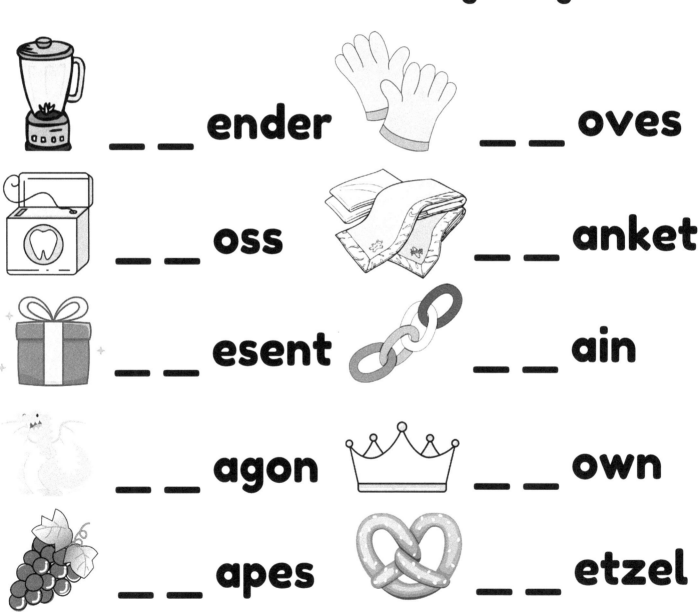

_ _ ender

_ _ oves

_ _ oss

_ _ anket

_ _ esent

_ _ ain

_ _ agon

_ _ own

_ _ apes

_ _ etzel

Letter Sounds

Say the name of each picture out loud and circle the beginning sound.

 d   j    h   b

 b   d   s   a

 t   s    c   b

 c   d    k   c

Rhyming Words

Circle the word that rhymes with the word inside the box.

| cat | bat | clap |

| pan | saw | can |

| bee | see | me |

| hand | land | bend |

| mop | lap | cop |

| lip | skip | drip |

1. Connect the picture to its digraph.
2. Complete the missing digraph to complete the word and draw a line to connect it.

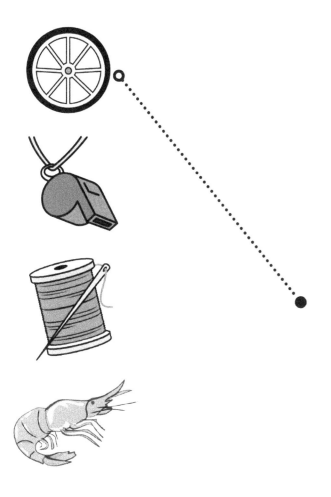

w h eel

_ _read

_ _rimp

_ _istle

_ _ick

_ _one

CONSONANT BLENDS

pr

pl

Fill in the blanks with the missing letters

☐ etzel

☐ ince

☐ ize

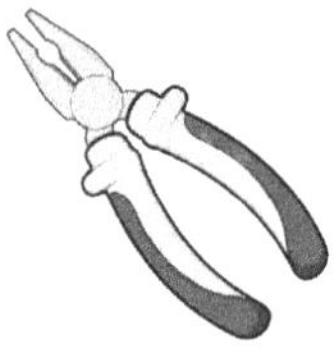

☐ ant

☐ iers

☐ anet

☐ incess

☐ iest

☐ ug

☐ umber

53

CONSONANT BLENDS

sc

sk

Fill in the blanks with the missing letters

[ ] hool

[ ] irt

[ ] i

[ ] ale

[ ] orpion

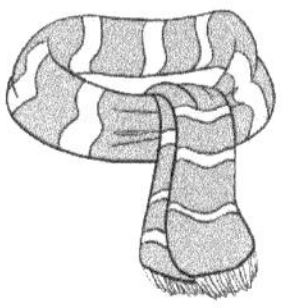

[ ] arf

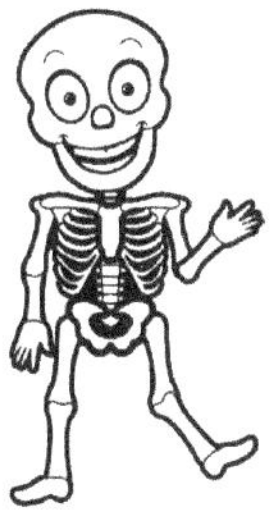

[ ] eleton

[ ] ateboard

[ ] ooter

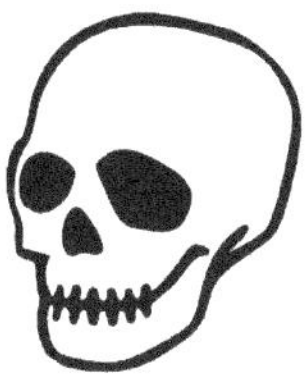

[ ] ull

Missing Middle

Choose the missing middle letter by making the sound of each letter in the choices.
Write the correct letter to complete the word.

l _ p

n _ t

p _ g

10

t _ n

w _ g

b _ d

Missing Middle

Choose the missing middle letter by making the sound of each letter in the choices.
Write the correct letter to complete the word.

CONSONANT BLENDS

Match to the picture to its beginning digraph

Picture Match

Circle the correct beginning sound of each picture.

   th   wh      sh   ch

   ch   ph      th   ph

   sh   th      ch   sh

   ch   wh      th   ph

58

I can READ
Simple Sentences

Read the sentences three times and match the
last word to its picture

I see the cat

I see the pan

I see the map

I see the bag

I see the bat

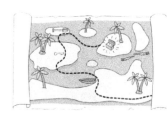

I see the fan

59

I can R&D
Sight Word Fluency

Read the sentences three times and match the
last word to its picture

It is sunny

It is cloudy

It is raining

It is lunch time

It is reading time

It is bedtime

I can **READ**
Sight Word Fluency

Read the sentences three times and match the
last word to its picture

The bird is blue
● ● ○

The cat is brown
● ● ○

The dog is black
● ● ○

The chick is yellow
● ● ○

The fish is red
● ● ○

The bear is white
● ● ○

61

SIGHT WORD HUNT

a

Find all the sight words and color them

a	does	after	a
after	a	does	a
a	does	a	after
a	after	does	a

SIGHT WORDS
FLUENCY CHECK

Read the sentence 3 times. Match the sentence to the correct picture

I see a boat

I see a mango

I see a bag

I see a cow

I see a house

I see a pen

I see a car

SIGHT WORD HUNT

an

Find all the sight words and color them

an	are	has	an
an	an	are	has
are	has	has	an
has	an	has	are

an

a c q v n p r z x
n a n b x a n d a
a c a n h o b l n
b w s a n h k t a
z a y t j a a n o
c n a b a n a u a
a n o p a n c a b

SIGHT WORDS FLUENCY

Read the sentences 3 times. <u>Underline</u> the sight words in the sentences.

He is an engineer.

There is an oven.

The man lives in an igloo.

There was an accident.

They planned an unexpected party

SIGHT WORDS
FLUENCY CHECK

an

Read the sentence 3 times. Match the sentence to the correct picture.

I see an ant

I see an orange

I see an octupus

I see an anchor

I see an egg

I see an owl

I see an umbrella

SIGHT WORD

all

Find all the sight words and color them.

am	be	all	be
all	am	be	all
be	all	be	am
all	am	all	be

SIGHT WORDS SEARCH

all

Find and circle the sight words

```
a b g h f p e z o
l x k b p a l l a
l c a l l c k j l
y g s a l l r n l
n a l l p b a l l
w q a h a l l c a
a l l o t n c h b
```

SIGHT WORD

Find all the sight words and color them.

is	he	is	that
that	is	that	he
he	is	is	he
is	that	he	that

SIGHT WORDS FLUENCY

Read the sentences 3 times. <u>Underline</u> the sight words in the sentences.

The dog is barking

The water is dripping

The blanket is wet

There is a new born baby

The beef is tender

SIGHT WORDS
FLUENCY CHECK

is

Read the sentence 3 times. Match the sentence to the correct picture. Circle the sight words.

The bus is big

The girl is pretty

The food is delicious

The phone is ringing

The boy is reading

The flower is red

The pillow is soft

SIGHT WORD

Find all the sight words and color them.

are	be	are	in
in	are	are	be
are	in	be	are
in	are	be	are

are

SIGHT WORDS
SEARCH

Find and circle the sight words

a r e t i d a r e
y a b p x a r e c
a h p o a r e l b
r w a r e d u e h
e a r e j a p n k
c n a r e n a r e
a r c p b l a r e

SIGHT WORDS

Read the sentences 3 times. <u>Underline</u> the sight words in the sentences.

The children are playing

The apples are on sale

The knives are sharp

The girls are pretty

The bags are packed

SIGHT WORDS
FLUENCY CHECK

Read the sentence 3 times. Match the sentence to the correct picture. Circle the sight words.

The pigs are pink

The grapes are fresh

The lizards are green

The birds are blue

The clothes are folded

The keys are colorful

SIGHT WORD HUNT

Find all the sight words and color them.

he	is	that	he
that	he	he	is
he	that	is	that
he	is	them	is

SIGHT WORDS
SEARCH

Find and circle the sight words

that

```
c b w t h a t r c
b q t h a t h k t
a t y a l r a l h
t h a t e d t e a
h a p e j a p n t
a t h a t n a r e
t r c p b t h a t
```

SIGHT WORDS FLUENCY

Read the sentences 3 times. <u>Underline</u> the sight words in the sentences.

That is his house

That is the canteen

That is her car

That tree is big

That is the entrance

SIGHT WORDS
FLUENCY CHECK

Read the sentence 3 times. Match the sentence to the correct picture. Circle the sight words.

Is that a fish?

Is that a boat?

Is that a mug?

Is that a notebook?

Is that a bicycle?

Is that a shell?

Is that a turtle?

SIGHT WORD
HUNT

after

Find all the sight words and color them.

and	after	and	so
so	and	and	after
and	after	after	so
after	and	so	after

after

SIGHT WORDS
SEARCH

Find and circle the sight words

p y a f t e r h n
s a f t e r c b f
a f t e r v u i d
j r e t a f t e r
x a r e b o s n k
p c h a f t e r e
t a f t e r h n l

SIGHT WORDS FLUENCY

Read the sentences 3 times. <u>Underline</u> the sight words in the sentences.

We ate ice cream after lunch

We took a bath after playing

I go to sleep after dinner time

I take vitamins after eating

I fix my toys after playing

SIGHT WORDS
FLUENCY CHECK

after

Read the sentence 3 times. Match the sentence to the correct picture. Circle the sight words.

I play basketball after school

I play football after school

I play volleyball after school

I play baseball after school

I play tennis after school

Sight Word Practice

find

Read it

find

Trace it

f i n d

Color it

find

Write it

We will _____ the missing puzzle piece

Sight Word Practice

little

Read it

little

Trace it

little

Color it

little

Write it

You are going to have a _____ sister.

Sight Word
Practice

from

Read it

from

Trace it

from

Color it

from

Write it

This book is _____ my dad.

87

Sight Word Practice

Read it

big

Trace it

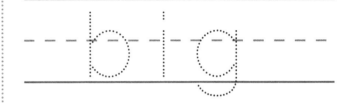

Color it

big

Write it

The house is _____

Sight Word Practice

Read it

Trace it

and

Color it

and

Write it

Sight Word Practice

all

Read it

all

Trace it

a l l

Color it

all

Write it

The new born kittens are _____ white.

Sight Word Practice

ate

Read it

ate

Trace it

ate

Color it

ate

Write it

The rabbits _____ all the carrots.

Sight Word Practice

by

Read it

by

Trace it

b y

Color it

by

Write it

Amie will go ____ train.

Sight Word Practice

Read it

fly

Trace it

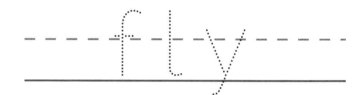

Color it

Write it

The birds can _____.

Sight Word Practice

Read it

do

Trace it

do

Color it

do

Write it

How ____ you feel right now?

Sight Word Practice

away

Read it

away

Trace it

a w a y

Color it

away

Write it

The girl looks _____.

95

Sight Word Practice

Read it

again

Trace it

again

Color it

again

Write it

It is raining _____

Sight Word Practice

Read it

have

Trace it

have

Color it

have

Write it

I _____ red mittens.

Sight Word Practice

Read it

we

Trace it

w e

Color it

we

Write it

Sight Word Practice

Read it

it

Trace it

i t

Color it

it

Write it

I want to wear ___ tonight.

Sight Word Practice

down

Read it

Trace it

d o w n

Color it

down

Write it

Other BrainChild books available on Amazon

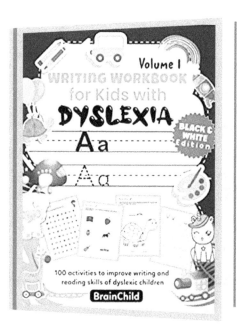

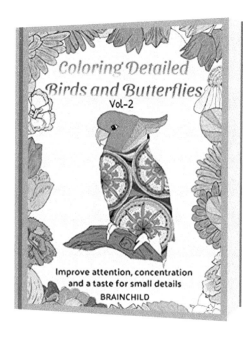